Accolades for Debby's Work

"I love the way you write!"

Dana Maloney

"Such a great writer! I love hearing you read stories and love your enthusiasm! Keep up the good work!"

Deborah McDonald

"Keep being more of you."

Willie Taylor

"Courageous, insightful and inspirational – a great read with plenty of photographs to draw you into the story."

John O'Melveny Woods

Debby Hackbarth

Dynamic Debby: Overcoming Prematurity and Poor Vision

Debby Hackbarth

Debby Hackbarth

ISBN: 978-1-961485-58-7 Paperback
ISBN: 978-1-961485-59-4 Hardback

FV-5

Published by:

Intellect Publishing, LLC

www.IntellectPublishing.com

Dedication

This memoir is dedicated the following:

- Those who have vision difficulties.
- Those who were born prematurely.
- Those who were bullied.

I understand your struggles. May this book be a source of inspiration to all who read it.

Little Debby, La Dueña Chica

vi

Debby Hackbarth

Author's Note

This memoir is a remarkable compilation of prose, poetry, and a plethora of precious photographs. It tells my story and it is meant to be an encouragement for all people who struggle with visual disabilities and low vision as well as those who are smaller than most through premature birth or heredity. The font used is best for folks with challenged vision.

Over the past several years, I have been able to gather photographs of my parents and their families. Many photos have already been passed onto our children and grandchildren. However, many remaining snapshots are included here to assist in telling my tale.

I have recalled stories and information to the best of my memory as both of my parents and their families have passed away. If I have made errors or misrepresentations, I apologize and hope you may gather inspiration from my trek through time.

Toward the end of the memoir, I mention Glisten, The Fairhope Dragon books. These books were created with illustrations from two of our grandsons and myself. The editing was done by family members and my publisher. You may purchase them online from Amazon or Barnes and Noble. For a closer look, please visit thefairhopedragon.com.

<u>Beholding Baby Glisten, The Fairhope Dragon</u>

<u>Gliding with Glisten, The Fairhope Dragon</u>

<u>Searching for Glisten, The Fairhope Dragon</u>

<u>The Glisten Trilogy Coloring Book</u>

Through my business, HAART, LLC, I sell tiny books to correlate with the Fairhope Dragon books, environment-focused booklets, and artwork. Contact me at: <u>dhackbarth7@gmail.com</u>.

Table of Contents

Preface

Some people prefer to tell tales about turbulent and troubled times. A few folks share terrific travels around our astounding sphere. Others choose to entertain those around them with delightful stories of their fantastic families.

My story is about a tiny preemie with low vision who should not have been born. May my journey give hope to others to rise above their circumstances and enjoy life to its fullest.

Perhaps we are only put on earth,

To try and find out where we fit in.

Maybe we are just part of a giant puzzle.

Hopefully, we are significant – each one of us.

No one will ever know.

Debby Hackbarth

Dynamic Debby: Overcoming Prematurity and Poor Vision

Debby Hackbarth

Prologue: A Tiny Tornado

My parents were desperate to have a child. They had been trying to have a baby for years. A few weeks after an initial miscarriage scare, their doctor them: "If you cannot get help for Lucille's excessive smoking; she will lose the baby."

Fortunately, a tiny tornado was born at three pounds, nine ounces, five weeks early. My body was positioned in a footling breech. The footling position is the worst of the four types of breech births. However, because I was tiny, the medical staff could turn me around for a normal birth.

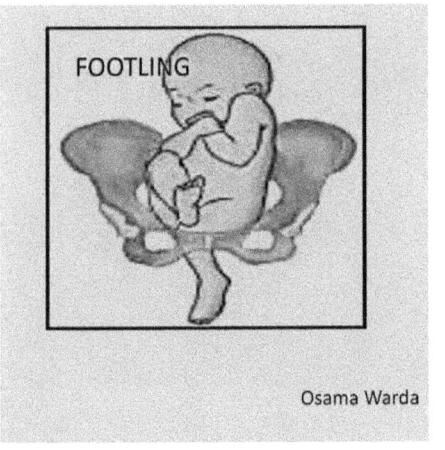

Osama Warda

I have always believed I was born to dance because I was a footling. In fact, I loved to tap dance, like my mother, who danced for many years. In her seventies, she danced in the elevators traversing eleven stories where she lived after she retired. This tall building in Oak Park, IL was close to the hospital where she and all her children were born. We would visit her at least once a month, like we had done for many years when she lived on Lake Michigan in downtown Chicago. Our kids named her "Grandma Train Tracks" because we paralleled the Northwestern tracks on our Grandma Journey.

My parents did not have the extra income for dance lessons. Fortunately, I danced in several performances in high school.

Glenbard East High in the 1960s

During West Side Story, in stilettos, I fell and broke my tail bone; while assisting the couples on stage. Because I delivered my children via C-Section, my tail bone did not fracture again.

In college, I enjoyed taking archery gymnastics, and creative dancing. Years later, I took tap lessons through the park district and eventually served as an assistant to my tap instructor. My petite stature never held me back from enjoying life.

I took dance lessons with my daughters, Bekah and Leah. Bekah and I performed two dances; one in penguin tees and one in homemade Santa outfits.

Years later, my left knee and left shoulder were injured in a car accident. This incident ended my tap dance instruction career, but I always hoped to dance again.

In 2019, I started to tap dance once more and hoped to be in the same recital as my granddaughter, a fifth-generation dancer. The Covid pandemic put the dream to rest. The recital was cancelled.

The dancing passion in my family was started with my maternal grandmother, Mae Lavin; continued with my mother; myself; my daughters; and my granddaughter. I am amazed at the fabulous dancing performed throughout the generations.

I won't let my lack of depth perception and low vision stop me from enjoying activities like archery, golf, and bicycle riding. I have great sense of rhythm and rarely can sit still; watch me dance for decades, like my mother did!

At the time of my birth, all premature babies were placed into oxygen chambers because many had underdeveloped lungs. One downside of this therapy caused my Retinopathy of Prematurity. This type of vision injury has caused many challenges in my life.

For the first month of my life, I lived in West Suburban Hospital, where my mom visited daily. Mother's milk and a strong sucking reflex kept me alive.

Through these portals life wends its way

West Suburban Hospital
Oak Park, Illinois

Created to Survive

Came five weeks early, created to survive,
Tiny like a mustard seed, ready to thrive.
Oxygen bolstered her lungs of little size,
Survival was more important than her eyes.

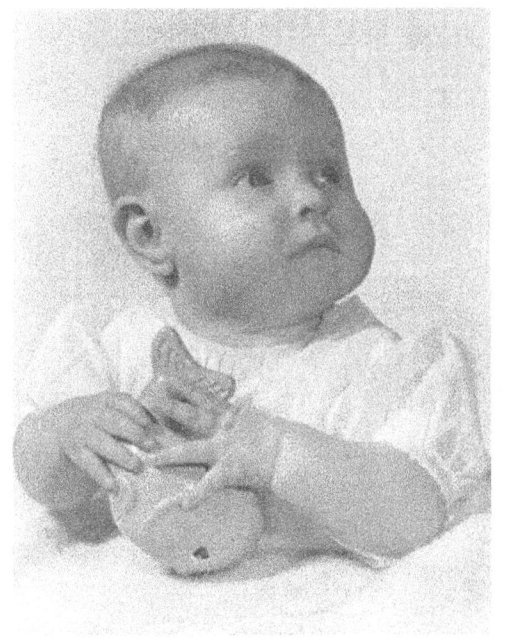

ENDURANCE, PERSISTENCE, DETERMINATION.

Mother's milk strengthened her in the hospital,

Love toughened her to never be second fiddle.

Born from a long line of fabulous females,

Leaders across decades, always blazing trails.

Grandma Ruby – Candy Striper

DANCERS, POETS, ARTISANS, TRAILBLAZERS

Weeks of nurses then months of sleepless nights,

Persevered through colic, boy did she fight!

This strenuous start sparked her stalwart self,

A tiny tornado, sure of herself.

Kindergarten

BEWARE, LOOK OUT, NEVER UNDERESTIMATE.

I created this sketch of my favorite toy for Glisten, the Fairhope Dragon books.

Chapter One: Grandmothers

The two women who were grandmothers to me were born in 1899 in Chicago. These wonderful ladies were drastically different, but equally talented women.

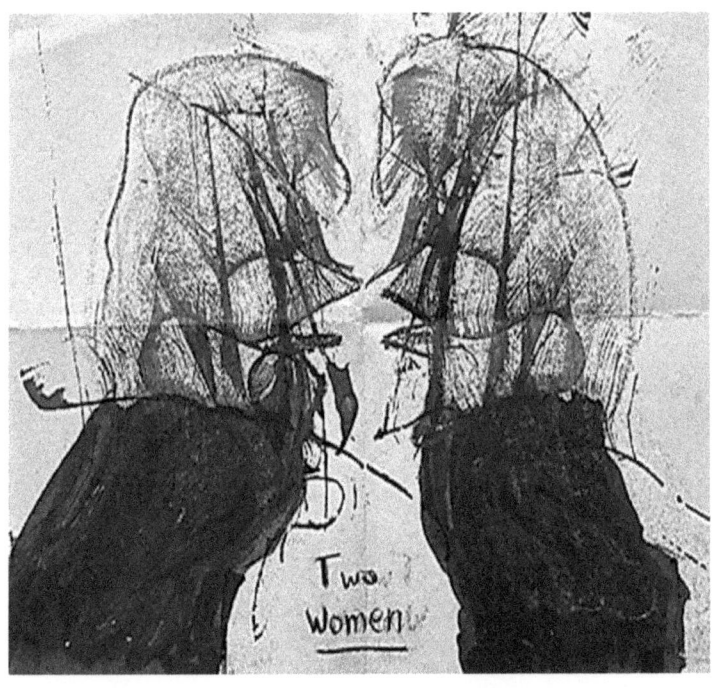

A fold-out sketch done in high school

Grandma Ruby – My Dad's Mother

Ruby made art from broken glass.

She gave us socks that glistened.

Dirty dishes would rarely pass.

But to her stories we listened.

Her home in Chicago was quite small.

Three rooms on each floor and a basement.

Rutherford Ave. in Chicago

The five of us didn't mind at all.
We wished our visits were more frequent.

One bathroom on the second floor.
We had to go upstairs alone.
"Don't open any other door."
This rule forced us to groan.

Bathroom journey, I was resolute.
I peered into her closet.
Shockingly, it was full of loot.
Tons of toilet paper, a safety net.

Ruby was passionate about art. I have two pieces of her glass wall art. I wish I had one of her tabletops decorated with mosaics of glass. She even painted the entire exterior of her Lark because she wanted a white vehicle!

Ruby also wrote poetry and passed the gift of writing onto myself and my grandson, Jonah.

Ruby moved to Grace Tower in CA to be close to her daughter. She loved the outdoors and continued to hike for many years.

GRACE TOWER
3955 Park Boulevard
San Diego, California 92103

Great Aunt (Grandma) Lucille Bernice – My Mom's Aunt

Lucille was a gentle soul.
Her laugh would fill a room.
Through her neighborhood we would stroll.
Smelling her sweet perfume.

She lived in a tiny space.
An apartment filled with smiles.
Freedom to explore her place.
It seemed to go on for miles.
One day I decided to explore.
Enchanted by her attire.
Old clothes in her closet quite a bore.
But jewelry I came to admire.

Lu wore lipstick every day.
Clip-on earrings to match her dress.
Blueberry pancakes on Sunday.
She favored me to excess.

My mother, Lucille, told me she opted to care for family members, instead of going to the university.

Lucille and Lucille Bernice

Lucille Bernice was married to a hard-working custodian, Jim. The couple lived on a meager salary in a teeny apartment. We enjoyed visiting because we could run around and watch her treasure, a television.

Jim, Lu, Great-Grandnephew - Dave

Lucille Bernice or Doo-Doo was devoted to her niece, Lucille. Lucille Bernice's nickname was created when I could not pronounce "Aunt Lu". Lucille Bernice doted on all of Lu's children.

Doo-Doo and tiny Debby

When my parents had a date night, I'd stay with Doo-Doo overnight. We'd eat blueberry pancakes and watch Bishop Sheen on Sunday morning television.

We had a great time together running errands and walking around her neighborhood. Daily, she would put on her lipstick and her clip-on earrings before heading outside. I loved her style!

walking the neighborhood

Chapter Two: My Parents

My parents, Ed and Lu, attended
Proviso High School in the Chicago
suburbs. To my knowledge, they did not
know each other in high school because
they were a few years apart.

Lu was active in school government and the theater. Ed participated in the marching band as an oboe player. He also played football

My mother's marriage to her first husband at the start of the war was annulled. The photo below was taken in 1943, during World War II, after she was available to date again.

They married in1946, four months
after my father's discharge from the Navy.

Ed and Lu were extroverts who loved being involved in volunteering opportunities, like hospital guild, PTA, and civil defense.

Their blustery marriage was filled with a plethora of proud moments and frequent fights. My mother needed to raise three decidedly different offspring by herself.

My father could not seem to find the perfect job. He moved through many different occupations and put in long hours. For example, while managing a gas station in Melrose Park; he worked seventy plus hours per week. He then transitioned to jobs in the insurance industry and the plumbing industry.

Unfortunately, my parents separated in 1969 at the end of my freshman year in college. Even though I was at college, I could hear the stress on the phone every time I called home. There was always screaming and shouting in the background. In 1970, my parents divorced and my father remarried four days later. Ed was married five times; however, my mother never remarried.

divorce deals devastating distress

Chapter Three: Edward LaVerne (1924)

Like my mother, my father was born and raised in Chicagoland during the Great Depression of the 1920s and the 1930s. Ed grew up in a nuclear family of four with his mother, Ruby, his father, Clyde, and his younger sister, Evelyn.

Ruby, Evelyn, and Clyde in 1929

Photos from the 1930s

According to my grandmother, Eddie loved being outside. He wanted to become a sailor one day. At the age of eighteen, his dream came true with the advent of World War II when he enlisted in the U.S. Navy.

Clyde in 1945

In his later years, Clyde developed liver disease. My grandmother told me he was sick because he had been kicked in the liver by his milk wagon horse.

Clyde spent many years in pain; however, it never stopped him from working every day. Ironically, Ed suffered from arthritis for many years, but he retired at the age of ninety-three. This fantastic work ethic has survived several generations.

Clyde served our country in the U.S. Marines and in the U.S. Army Infantry in World War I. My dad often mentioned the pride he felt for his dad's devotion to our country.

Both Ed and Clyde stood about 5'8";
however, they served the country they
loved as proud giants.

Clyde and Ed in 1943

Ed served in his country as a
Second-Class Sonar Man on the U.S.S.
Raven, a mine sweeper.

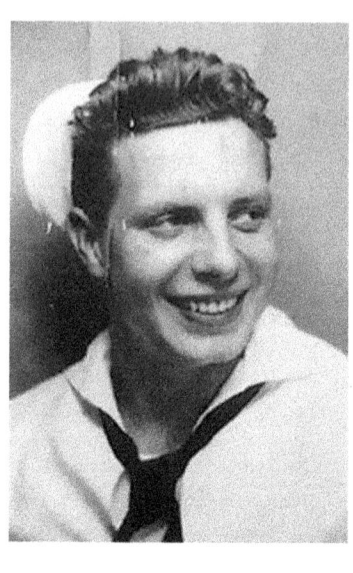

Below is a sketch of the U.S.S. Raven we proudly display in our living room, in his honor.

Ed told us a story about serving in the Philippines when sailors standing guard around him were killed. In another incident, he heard an enemy soldier breathing behind him. Fortunately, the man was called away and Ed was not wounded. While in Southeast Asia; he fought malaria, pink eye, impetigo, and trench mouth, all at the same time.

Edward was honorably discharged from the U.S. Navy with a dependency exemption in March, 1946 because his father died. During the war, Ruby worked part-time as a seamstress and had a limited income. Ed came home from the war to take care of her.

An extremely proud moment in both of our lives occurred on 9/26/2011. Ed was honored as a Knight or Chevalier in the French Army, for his involvement in the landing at Omaha Beach during World War II.

Like many folks who serve our nation, my dad came back from the war with PTSD. My mom told us stories about how he would dive under the table, whenever he heard loud sounds. He also had a hearing loss from the large guns on his ship and wore hearing aids later in life.

Unfortunately, I did not know my father very well. He worked many long hours throughout most of my childhood because he was the main breadwinner. My mother did not work, like many women in the 1950s and 1960s.

He was present at important events like the wedding of one of his cousins when my sister and I served as flower girls. As I grew up, he enjoyed watching me act in many theatrical performances. In his later years, he repeatedly stated he was proud of me.

He moved to Florida in his mid-sixties because he loved warm weather and fast boats. We visited him whenever we could and he did not travel north very often. We all missed him and I called him frequently.

Most of the family traveled to Florida for his 90th surprise birthday celebration. He was totally shocked and loved talking, laughing, and dancing with folks at the party. He said the highlight of the party was seeing his great grandchildren.

Reluctantly, he retired at ninety-three. He had survived a world war, a heart valve replacement and throat/tongue cancer in his eighties. He was an intelligent and hard-working salesman who was married five times to five beautiful women. He only had children with my mother.

We visited him two weeks before his death mid-June in 2019 for Father's Day. We celebrated our wedding anniversary at his home.

Tragically, two weeks later, we arrived at his home; fifteen minutes after his death. I closed his eyes and kissed his forehead. His celebration of life was held close to his 95th birthday. Our son, Dave, gave the eulogy and I read a Bible verse at this event.

Every year on June 6th, Dave, posts this collage in honor of his grandfather. It shows the following: the landing on Utah Beach on June 6, 1944; a picture of Ed as a young sailor; Ed holding Dave as a newborn; Dave's graduation from high school; and Dave honoring Ed at Ed's funeral service in July of 2019.

Chapter Four: Lucille Mae (1921)

Lu was named after her aunt, Lucille Bernice. My mother lost her mother, Mae, when she was two years old.

This photo shows Mae holding John with her sisters Lucille Bernice and Catherine by her side. Mae's twin sister, Genieve, died very young and the family lost their only son, John, when he was a baby.

Mae and Lucille had crossed eyes. This condition is known as strabismus. I don't know if they had amblyopia or a "lazy eye" as well. These traits are common in other members of our family. In addition to strabismus and amblyopia, I have Retinopathy of Prematurity (ROP) or Retrolental Fibroplasia. Mae was diminutive and Lu was born about five weeks early, like me; but I don't know if they had ROP.

Mae died from an infection, when she was twenty-five years old. Her family did take her to the hospital, but it was too late. Ironically, the main cause of my mother's death stemmed from an infection.

Lu's father, Fred, took off grief-stricken and left his son and daughter alone. Lu was raised by her widowed grandmother, Effie. The church took pity on Effie and Lu and allowed them to live in the rectory.

Fred's first wife's family took care of her half-brother, Bob. Tragically, Lu never saw Bobby again; even though Lu did search for him when she was older.

Lucille

Bob

Both Lucille, known as Baby Lu, and Mae stood about five feet tall. I never found out if Mae was premature; however, she was a tiny lady. Her framed beaded flapper dress hangs in our home. It was made for someone of petite stature.

Because Mae's small hands were beautiful, she had the opportunity to model them. I was asked to model my lovely hands as well. I had three small children at the time and chose not to leave them for long hours or take them with me to work in Chicago.

self-portrait of my hands

A wealthy friend of the family doted on Baby Lu and gave her opportunities few others her age or social status obtained. This kind man arranged for Lucille to do some professional modeling; enrolled her in the Miss Dairy Beauty Contest; and arranged for her to take horseback riding lessons.

Lucille modeling

Lucille and Effie

Lucille excelled at horseback riding, despite her teeny stature. She enjoyed going to equestrian events throughout her lifetime.

This passion for horseback riding was passed to me and Leah; who rode and jumped using an English saddle. The saddle below is a tribute to the riders in the family.

Effie, Lu's guardian, was well-loved and respected by her friends and family. Effie's heritage goes back to kings and queens in England and Scotland; even though Effie's father was born in Sweden. Other family members were born in New York, but the entire family settled in the Chicago suburbs.

Effie and her sister Ella (1936)

Family rallied around Lu and Effie
and frequently took them to cabins on Paw
Paw Lake in MI and to Lake Marie in IL.

Lu (1937)

Doo-Doo and Baby Lu with family at Lake Marie

My family and I went to the Michigan Dunes many times throughout the years. We took our children to Lu's trailer on a lake in WI often.

Deb – MI Dunes (1950s)

My mom grew up on the lakes. Later in life, she took up sailing. This passion to spend time on the water continues in the lives of her children, grandchildren, and great-grandchildren.

Lucille Mae was a popular and confident extrovert. She was involved in school activities such as student government and theater

She chose to attend secretarial school instead of going to college, so that she could take care of Effie.

Lu and Effie

When her marriage failed, she took a job as an executive secretary. I was proud of her when she remembered her shorthand notations from high school! While working at Sears Tower she had the opportunity to act in several commercials. Acting during high school paved the way for this privilege. Her tiny stature and low vision did not hold her back

My mother's death was caused by infection induced septic shock and pneumonia. She died in September of 2004 in the hospital; after living in a nursing home for years.

When I inherited her scrapbook; I realized she was a poet and collector of articles on child psychology. I am proud of Baby Lu, who overcame poverty and adversity. At her funeral, many people gave testimonies as to how she had positively impacted their lives.

Often there are not enough hours,

To enjoy precious moments,

With those we love.

Debby Hackbarth

Chapter Five: Prematurity-Smoking

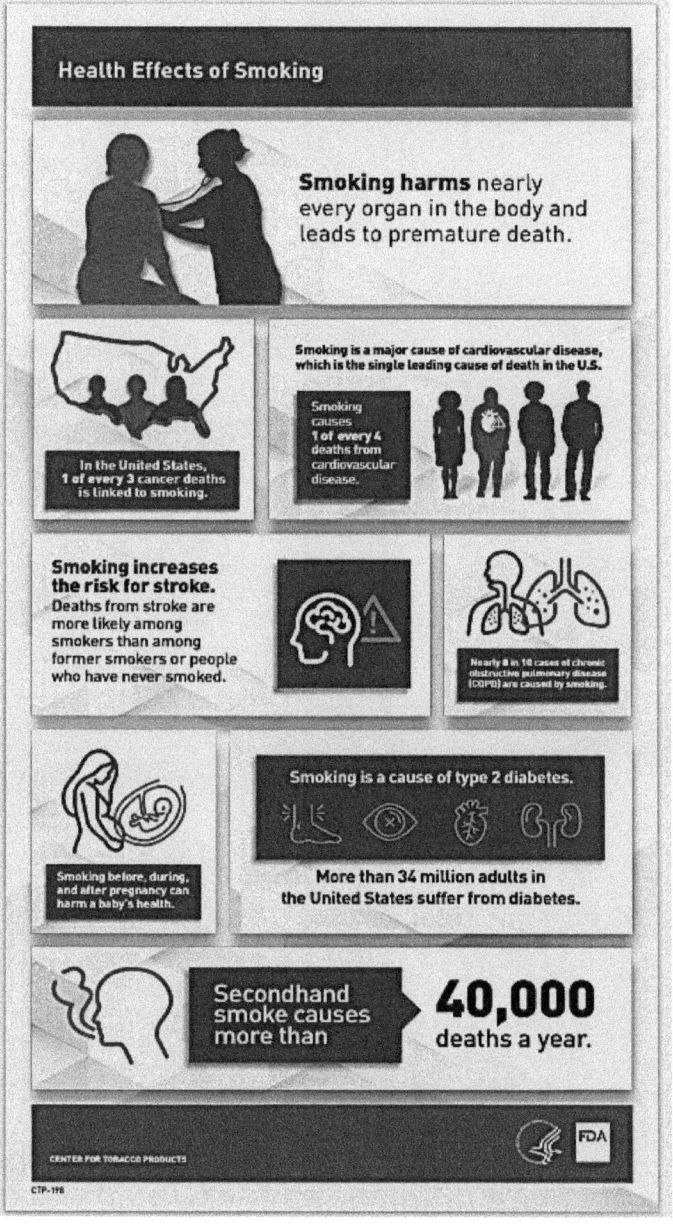

Research has linked cigarette smoking with miscarriage and low birth rate. Heavy smoking involves twenty-five to thirty cigarettes per day, according to the National Institute of Health. Lucille smoked about three packs a day or fifty to sixty "cancer sticks"; even when she was on oxygen.

For years, Lu had emphysema, a disease where the air sacs of the lungs are damaged; usually by smoking. Often, this ailment leads to pneumonia. Various factors, including pneumonia caused by emphysema, contributed to her death. Emphysema ruined her lungs and her ability to pump oxygen to her brain. At the end of her life, this lack of oxygen caused asphyxia dementia.

Unfortunately, my father smoked as well throughout his life. He started with cigarettes during the war. In fact, the armed forces gave cigarettes to the servicemen. He smoked pipes for decades. His smoking caused tongue/throat cancer, which he overcame. However, it damaged his quality of life because he constantly coughed during his meals to dislodge food stuck in his throat.

Our homes were always filled with smoke, which was not great for our health. Cigarette smoking was one cause of my premature birth. I suffered from frequent bronchitis during my life, probably caused by second hand smoke. I was often embarrassed about the way my clothes smelled when I went to school. Plus, the ugly tar in the cigarettes stained our curtains, carpeting, and damaged artwork

My mother was a kind and beautiful woman who started smoking at seventeen and stopped around the age of eighty, only because the nursing home would not allow smoking in the facility. My handsome father quit many years before the cancer hit him. The damage had already been done.

I was going through pictures of my mother. Most of the photos showed Lu smoking. Because her smoking habit contributed to her suffering and death; now most of the photos in my collection show her without a cigarette. I threw out many cigarette-related photos out of grief.

The following photographs are the only pictures I have with my mom holding a cigarette.

If you currently smoke or vape or know someone who does smoke or vape; please find a way to quit and help others to quit as well. Nicotine is extremely addicting and ultimately it can cause you and your loved ones to suffer.

The resources below may assist you in finding more information on how you may help someone you care about stop smoking. Please research them and contact your favorite medical professional for help, before it's too late.

https://www.ncbi.nlm.nih.gov/pmc/articl es/PMC3969532/

https://www.cdc.gov/tobacco/campaign/ tips/quit-smoking/index.html

https://www.webmd.com/smoking- cessation/ss/slideshow-13-best-quit- smoking-tips-ever

https://my.clevelandclinic.org/health/arti cles/17488-smoking

https://www.betterhealth.vic.gov.au/heal th/healthyliving/pregnancy-and-smoking

My mother's addictions negatively impacted the births of all three of her children.

brother - almost died at birth

sister – under five pounds at birth

Chapter Six: Prematurity-Alcohol

In an article by the National Institute of Health, it states: "In one study (Kesmodel et al. 2000), consumption of 10 or more drinks per week was associated with a nearly threefold increase in the risk of delivery prior to 37 weeks". Both of my parents were heavy drinkers most of my childhood. I recall seeing them drinking every night. When they wanted to diet, they would switch from beer to whisky and water.

I was born five weeks early after three near miscarriages and my sister and I both had very low birth weights. In an article by National Health Service, it states: "Drinking alcohol during pregnancy increases the risk of miscarriage, premature birth and your baby having a low birthweight. It can also affect your baby after they're born."

These resources may help you to understand the link between drinking alcohol, low birth rate, and prematurity.

https://www.ncbi.nlm.nih.gov/pmc/articl es/PMC3860553/#:~:text=In%20one%20s tudy%20(Kesmodel%20et,significantly% 20associated%20with%20preterm%20de livery.

https://www.nhs.uk/pregnancy/keeping-well/drinking-alcohol-while-pregnant/#:~:text=Drinking%20alcohol% 20during%20pregnancy%20increases,al cohol%20spectrum%20disorder%20(FA SD).

Chapter Seven: My Early Years

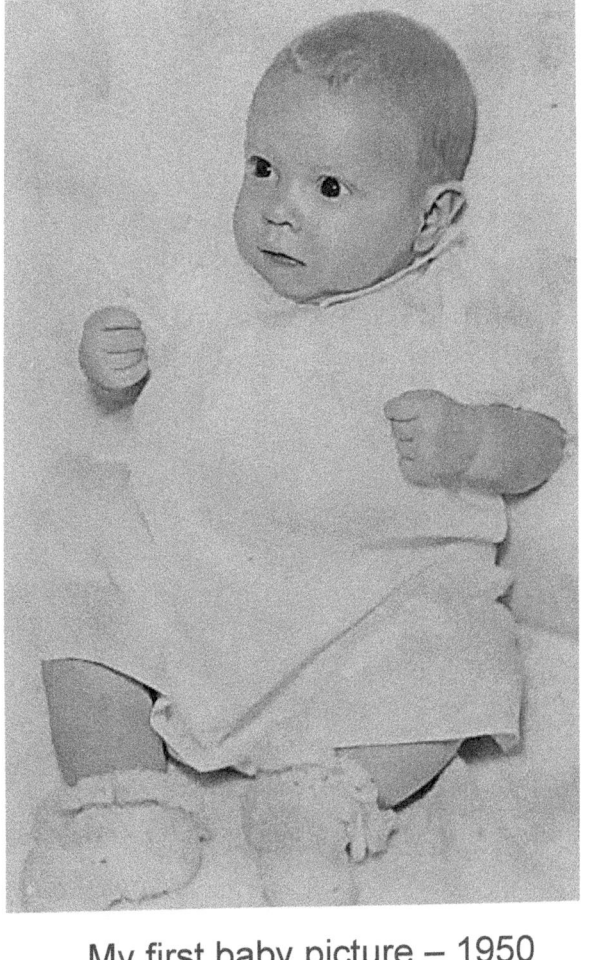

My first baby picture – 1950

Disorganized and abnormal blood vessels grew on the retinal tissues at the back of my left eye before I was born.

Due to amblyopia, I have grown up with a loss of depth perception and night blindness. Unless my brain "turns off" my left eye, I have double vision. I needed to "turn it on" to complete a test to obtain my driver's license. The examiner did not understand. Later in life, I could have retinal detachment, macular degeneration or complete blindness.

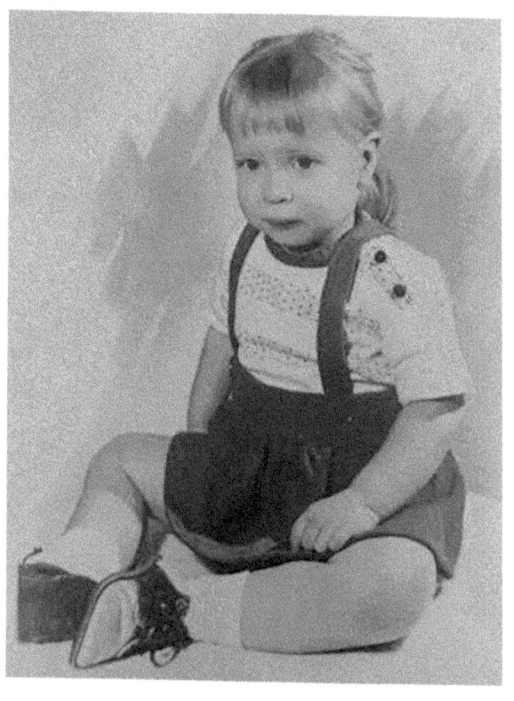

When my eye doctor showed me pictures of my retinas, the left one was pink and my right was red. According to a report from my doctor: "Her ocular history is positive for Retinopathy of Prematurity (ROP), strabismus and amblyopia in her left eye." I needed to use this information at several jobs because I could not satisfy some requirements due to my disability.

To this day, I struggle with staying happy. When you are much smaller than everyone else and cannot see anything on your left side; life can be very difficult.

For better or worse, my parents were over-protective and I sought to please them constantly. It took years to learn I need to be happy with myself before I can please others.

Support from my husband, children, friends, and unconditional love from my pets has comforted me through the years.

my favorite place: nature

Encouragement can emanate from anyone.

*Committed care was a constant
companion.*

This I will never forget – "best things come in small packages".

REALIZE REALITY

RESOUNDS WITH

RADIANCE!

Reassurance resounds from loved ones.

PRAISE – EXPECTATIONS

EXPRESSIONS – GESTURES

Chapter Eight: Time for School

Fortunately, my parents sought vision professionals for me at three years old. I started Kindergarten at four years old wearing glasses. The vision care I needed was difficult for my family because we survived on a modest income. We lived in a tiny home in a small village in the Midwest.

During visual therapy, I traced figures while looking into the Cheiroscope at the doctor's office. This activity helped my eyes to get stronger and to work together.

Single Oblique Stereoscope (Cheiroscope)

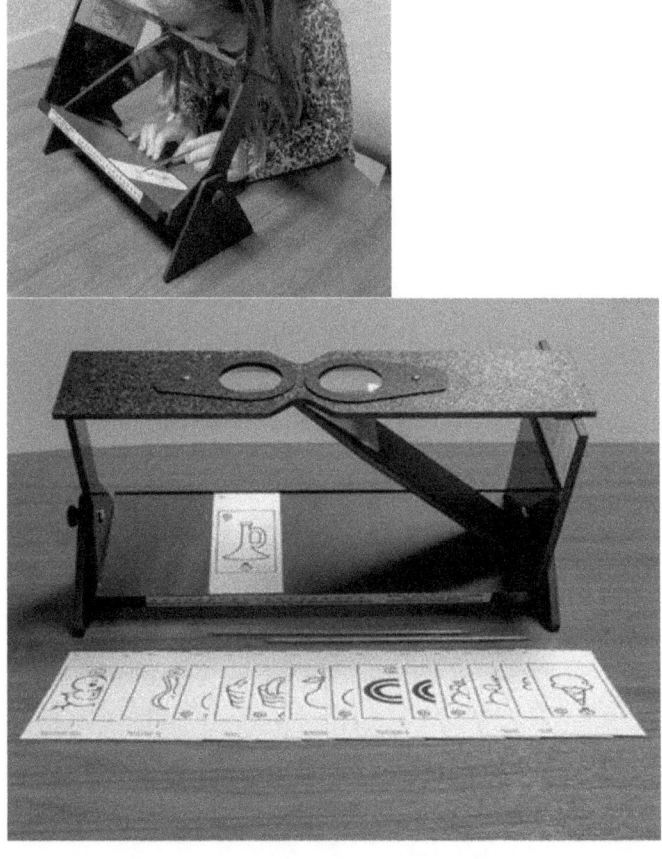

The summer before school started, my father put blocks onto my tricycle pedals to help me ride. There was no stopping me!

I started school with a patch over my right eye, so that my left eye could be strengthened. The doctors told my parents the lens in my glasses would straighten my eye as well as improve my vision. The surgery to correct amblyopia was dangerous at the time.

The patch on my right eye kept me from seeing well enough to read. I was the only student in my grade who wore glasses. I was subject to constant bullying.

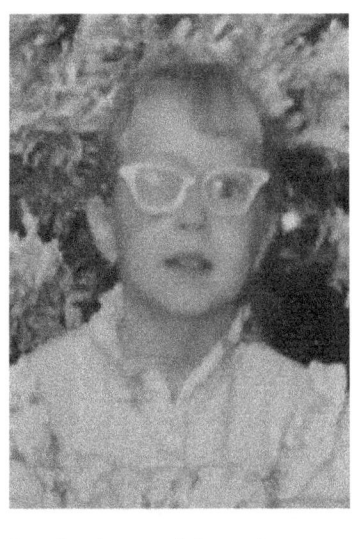

The students loved to place me at the end of "crack the whip" to see the little one "with one eye" fly off the end. The best part of my day occurred when my teacher played the piano in class during nap time.

I could not zipper my coat or fasten the clips on my boots or galoshes. My eyes did not work together in tandem to allow me to line up these tasks. Some students would laugh at my struggles.

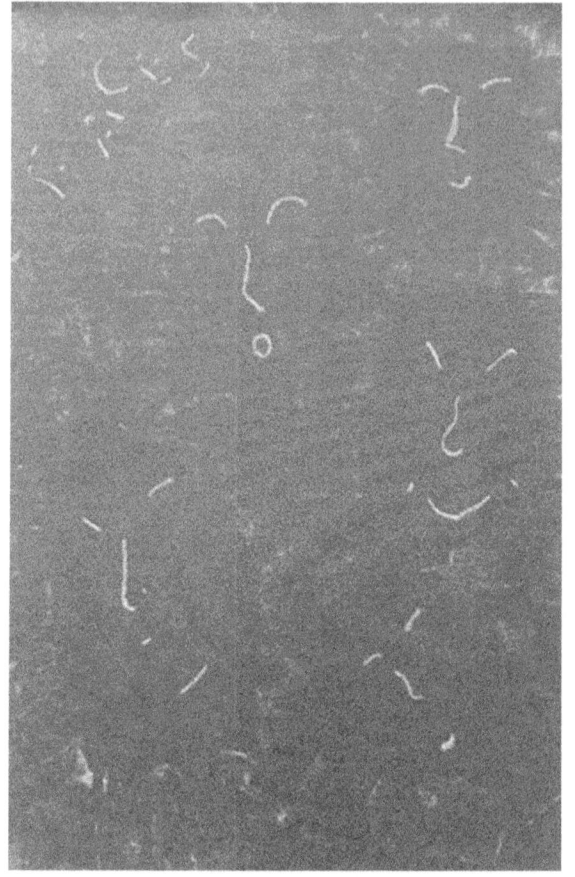

Critical faces always watching.

The girl next door, who knew about my vision difficulties, liked to bully me. She knew I could see very little on my left side. One day, she snuck up on me and hit me with a metal rake. It actually stuck out of my head for a short time! My mother spoke sternly with her mother and our friendship with the family was damaged.

As an adult, I had visual therapy again. The therapy included looking at pictures with special glasses and holding a beaded string to help my eyes to align. When the therapy ended, he doctors stated the vision in my left eye would probably never improve. They stressed the therapy I received as a young child, probably saved the vision in my left eye. I hope my right eye is never damaged.

The optometrists did have a program to help children with their reading skills. They hired me to work there. I enjoyed helping children who had visual challenges improve their reading.

I am grateful I have been able to play piano throughout the years; even though I have difficulty coordinating my hands with my eyes. My parents bought an upright piano and I took lessons for two years.

Piano sessions were a challenge because my teacher shouted at me when I could not perform to her standards. Sadly, my father lost his job and we needed to sell the piano.

Years later, my husband and I bought a used piano from a neighbor. All of our children took lessons on this Wurlitzer before they started playing other instruments in the school band. Playing the piano was a good foundation for them and a pleasure for me.

I was able to resume lessons in my thirties. My outstanding teacher encouraged me to memorize one song for a private recital. The task was difficult; however, I welcomed the challenge. We were unaware of all of my visual and reading challenges.

When my husband and I moved from TX to AL; we sold the piano to the family of one of my students. After moving to AL, Jim bought me a used baby grand piano! He saw how distraught I was after selling the piano we had cherished for years.

I found an awesome piano teacher in my own neighborhood, Toni. She has become a fabulous, forever friend. We socialize frequently with her and her husband, Henry.

She's a preemie, breathing is first.

Nobody expected the worst.

Some tiny ones were born blind.
I could see, so life was kind.

Doctors decided to incubate,
No care if eyes couldn't tolerate.
Lungs were fine, but vision damage,
No one foresaw the years of torment.

School days brought pain, ridicule.
Very few showed the golden rule.
Shouts of "4 eyes" sent me crying.
Sheer willpower kept me flying.

Weeks early, I appeared foot-first,
Due to the rules, I was reversed.
Little tow head with crossed eyes.
Didn't know she'd later rise.

How do you mend from maltreatment?

How do you transform from tragedy?

How do you counteract cruelty?

Continue to contemplate outside the norm.

Celebrate life with pride in yourself.

Color outside the lines.

Break out!

I started first grade behind my peers scholastically, but my ability to communicate and entertain others helped me to survive. I do remember, during the first two years of school being carried to the principal's office for talking too much.

I ran home many days in tears; after students shouted "Four Eyes" to my face. This I will never forget: "you can't do it". I defied everyone and continued to believe I could do whatever I chose to do, with boundless energy!

IDEAS IGNORED

DREAMS DASHED

PLANS PARALYZED.

TOUGH SCHOOL DAYS.

PERSERVERENCE

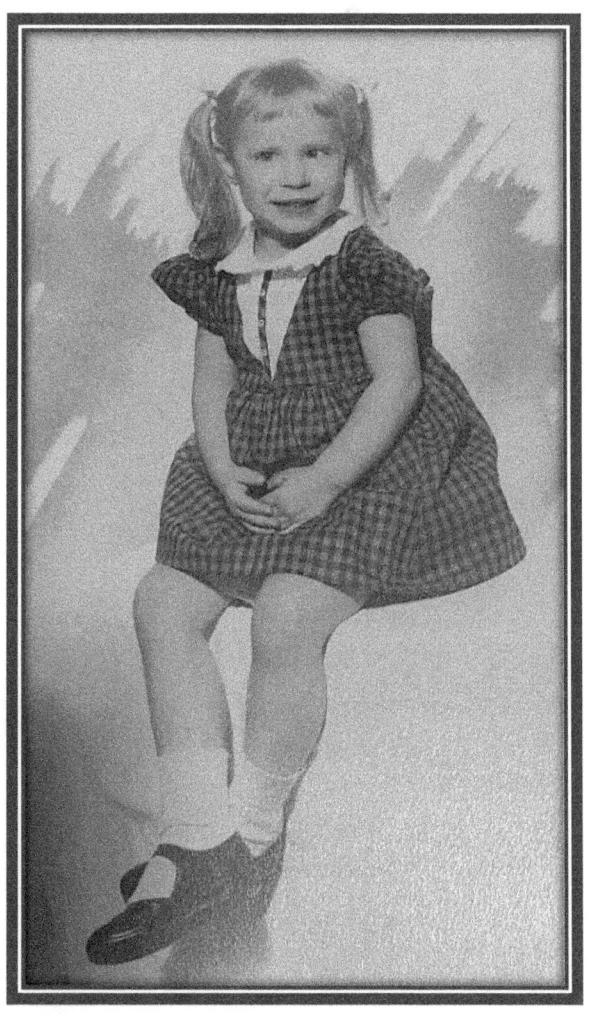

My best friend, Kathy, helped me to keep going. She walked home with me every day. We were close friends for many years; even after she cut off my pony tail to my delight and to my mother's dismay. We have connected again in our senior years.

In third grade, Mrs. Osborn helped me to be a successful reader and to tell time. Feeling confident, I wrote my first skit, to my family's delight.

During my fourth-grade year, my mother placed me into a pilot after-school Spanish program. I loved the language and the people. I was the champion of the marbles game tournament and had my first crush on a boy. I enjoyed swimming immensely. My father's nickname for me was Fish. Little Debby was finally blossoming!

Chapter Nine: Middle Grades

When my father was on a hunting trip with our neighbor, he was severely injured. He flew through the windshield and then recoiled back into the car. I saw him cry for the first time, when he walked through the door of our small Cape Cod style house. He told us he cried because he did not expect to see his children again.

With the money from the settlement, we were able to relocate to a lovely brick home in a more affluent neighborhood. This move made my mother very happy.

My fifth-grade year was arduous because I was not reading at grade level. I did aid a classmate who was always being bullied due to his size and his name. I had endured years of abuse and was ready to help someone else overcome adversity.

There was joy in my life. Hours were filled with piano playing; Spanish lessons on television; and the anticipation of theater in junior high. I adored having Suzy and her puppies around! Animals give unconditional love. I don't need to "prove myself" to them; just love them back.

Doo-Doo, Deb, Suzy

My portrait of Suzy

Sometimes life seems cruel. When everything seemed marvelous, my parents lost the house. We moved with three newborn puppies, no piano, and a very unhappy mother. The home environment was stressful due to low income and a troubled marriage. On a positive note, a fascinating home was in our future. My family moved into the Knippen farmstead, which contained an apple orchard.

The house was over one-hundred years old and my mother was hopeful we would be able to buy it. She decorated the farmhouse in shades of apple green. She consulted with a paint expert because her vision, like mine, could not differentiate between hues.

It was a busy time settling in with a litter of puppies; harvesting apples for treats; selling lilacs from the property; and exploring the cellar of the house. In the cellar was a door had been cemented shut. This door led to a tunnel which was used to help slaves escape during the Civil War!

Illinois countryside

My parents saw my love for people of all cultures. They were thrilled when Lincoln Elementary School started a pilot program in Spanish after school. I enjoyed teaching Spanish to my stuffed animals and siblings.

Later, my parents enrolled me in ponytail league baseball as well as tennis. Due to my size and my vision challenges; it was amazing I could perform these sports. I continued taking tennis lessons for years.

One of my tennis coaches became an elementary principal at the school I attended, Pleasant Lane. After college, I substitute taught there!

In addition, I played baseball in ponytail league as a catcher, with a mouth full of braces. One afternoon, as I waited for my parents to pick me up, an old man exposed himself to me. This act of bullying and intimidation was unforgivable. We took him to court; however, he was released. His wife said he was not feeling well!

My mother acted in high school and saw the same gift in me. Lombard Junior High School started a theater program and I was eager to join! My outgoing and dramatic personality was a perfect fit.

During one performance, I sat on the edge of the stage and spoke to the audience. I absolutely loved performing in this fashion. My friends and family were amazed at my confidence as a novice actress!

Until you perform in front of a live audience; you'll never understand the fantastic vibes present between an actor and the audience. In my opinion, this relationship may be the reason many actors return to the theater, after having a career in motion pictures.

Like every budding actor, I hoped to act on Broadway or in movies, but I never moved to Hollywood or New York City. As an adult, I did act in community theater; wrote skits; and directed church events.

Lombard is the Lilac Town,

A famous spot of renown.

Living in a tiny Cape Cod,

To the five of us, it wasn't odd.

Chicagoland

Two girls, one boy shared one room.

Siblings of the baby boom.

One bathroom for five wasn't too bad.

Having our own back yard made us glad.

Outside

School came at the age of four.

Bullying made the fun, a chore.

No one wore glasses in my class.

Being "4 eyes" was just too crass.

Eyepatch

Dad's accident gave us money.
This made Mom's life very sunny.
A brick house in a fancy locale.
PTA president, quite the gal.

Socialites

Instead of an air strip for us to hike.
We explored for hours, what's not to like.
As time went on, we lost the house.
Mom was unhappy with her spouse.

Conflict

High school was bursting with good times.
Honors classes, theater lines.
Tiny Debby, ready for college.
Leaving home, acquiring knowledge.

Freedom

Chapter Ten: High School

Like my grandmother, Ruby, I loved to draw. Even now, drawing gives me a sense of peace.

The sketch above was difficult to execute because I have no depth perception.

I started working in the theater department in my freshman year. I helped in the construction of the stage and the backdrops. The play was *The Diary of Anne Frank*. It was thrilling to watch the set unfold!

My entire high school path was filled with all aspects of theater arts from acting, to box office work, and serving as the Assistant Director on The Crucible. This position is the highest honor a thespian at the high school level can achieve. Plus, I adored working with Mrs. Meyer and enjoyed being in a leadership position.

TRYOUTS FOR

"THE CRUCIBLE"

Mon., Sept. 18 through Fri., Sept. 22

2:30 P.M. ON... ROOM 310

ALL STUDENTS WELCOME

Working at various roles in the theater; no one bullied me for my crossed eye and my thick glasses. They appreciated me for the talented person who "gave it her all" when doing any task handed to her. Theater was my passion!

Eagerly, I built up five-hundred hours of theater work. I planned to start college with a double major in Spanish and Theater. Having been in two honors classes in high school; I was accustomed to long hours of difficult work.

Together with a few friends, we started a drama club. We selected yellow and red as our colors and my mother sewed dresses for us. We held fundraisers to help promote the National Thespian Society; now known as the International Thespian Society.

One of my theater friends planned a blind date between my future husband and myself. He knew Jim from athletics and knew me from working on plays. At my twentieth high school reunion, several people were amazed I was not a movie star. I told them I fell in love and the rest was history.

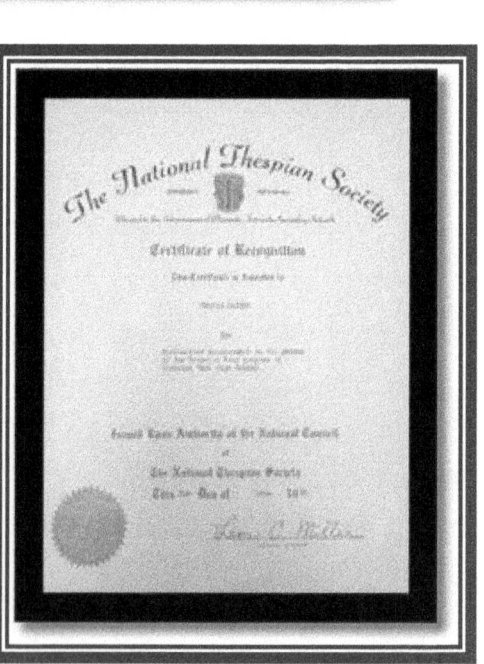

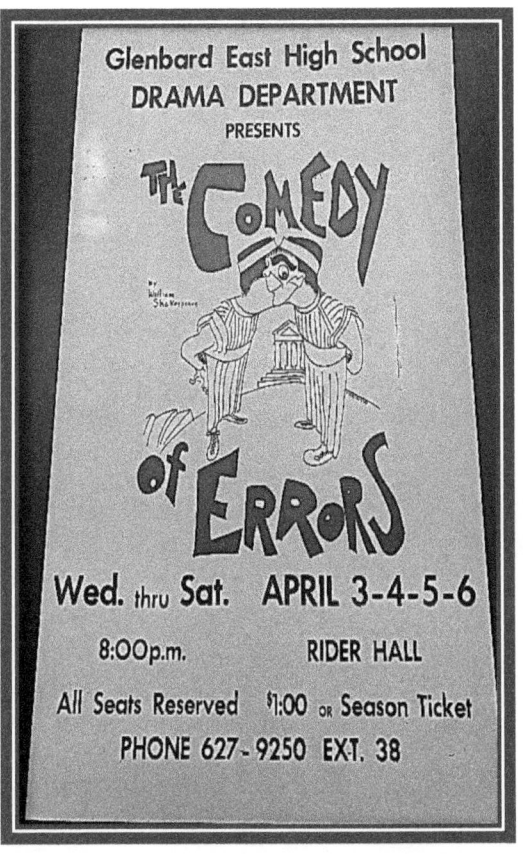

This Shakespearean play was performed on a slanted stage. My role was a purple-colored witch. At one point, I ran down the stage toward the audience. My father was shocked; he stood up to catch me during the performance!

I adored being in this performance as I was able to sing and dance. Later, I performed in an adaptation of *West Side Story* in stilettos!

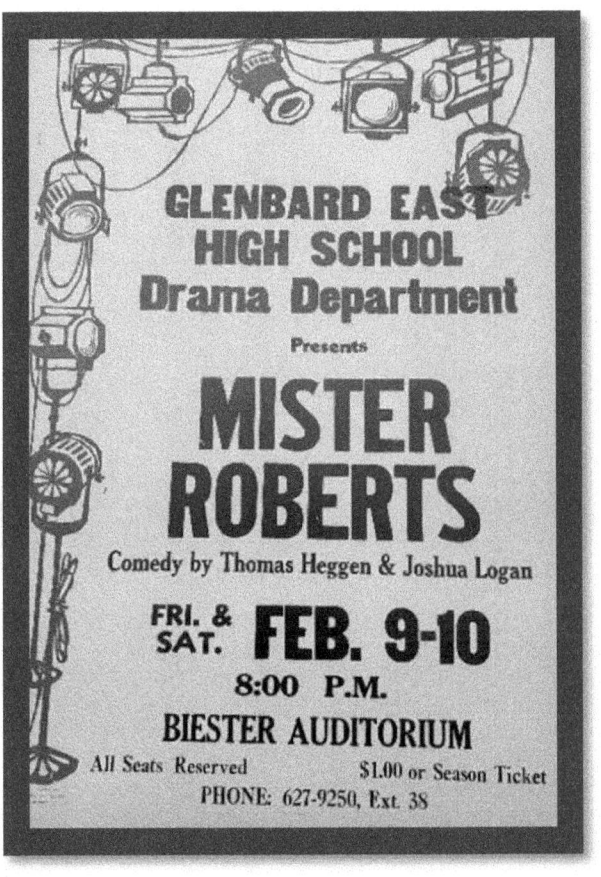

For *Mister Robers*, I led the advertising team. My parents said I needed a break from the extreme time commitment of acting. To keep me healthy, they dissuaded me from trying out for *The Music Man*.

Being an extrovert, I enjoyed
socialization and loved dressing up.

Western Illinois University (WIU) is located in Macomb, surrounded by farmland.

Chapter Eleven: College

Because of my good grades and work in the theater; I received a scholarship and a grant to attend WIU. This college had the reputation of having the best theater program in the state. After testing, I received two years of college Spanish and proceeded to take every higher-level Spanish class. I was excited to leave home and start my own life.

In my freshman year, I lived in a new dorm – Higgins Hall. I was fortunate to have roommates from my high school. My second roommate and I both suffered from eye fatigue. This challenge did not stop us from studying for many hours and achieving great grades.

As a child, I wanted to be a fire fighter or a professional pianist. As I grew up, my parents steered me toward teaching. In today's world, foreign language majors are guided toward the business world. As this was my first time away from home, I created a large calendar on the back of a box to help me stay focused.

All students at WIU needed to take classes in physical education. My choices included archery, creative movement or dance, and gymnastics. The gymnastics team asked me to join them because I showed promise. However, a bad accident during finals damaged my neck and mid-back. I needed to end gymnastics. Chiropractic medicine helped me tremendously.

At the end of my first year when my mother picked me up for summer break; she told me my father had left the family. This situation saddened me, but I heard the tension in the family every time I called home. I was not surprised at her news.

Even though my family life became even more turbulent; I continued to excel in college and made the Dean's List many times. The academic environment suited me and I studied on average five hours per night. To balance all of the studying, I did find time to have some fun; especially with my best friend, Lynn.

Lynn and I met in the theater and remain friends today.

I was not able to spend my junior year studying in Spain, due to the divorce. Fortunately, during the summer of 1971, I enrolled to study at the University of San Francisco in Guadalajara, Mexico. To celebrate the upcoming trip, Jim and I reconnected and Lynn, Jim, and I went out for ice cream.

The trip to Mexico was my first time on an airplane and my first time out of the country. The only scary time was a rough landing, in bad weather coming into Mexico. The plane was filled with screaming women and children.

On a field trip during the summer, I visited Teotihuacan. I was thrilled to visit the Pyramid of Quetzalcoatl!

I studied advanced Spanish grammar and Mexican art and lived in the suburban home of a widow and her daughter. Two girls from California were my roommates. The food was fantastic and the widow brought me to a baptism party for a relative in downtown Guadalajara.

The family's home was a hallway with bedrooms to one side separated by blankets for walls. There was an elevated kitchen area at the end of the hall. The only bathroom was a closet without a door with a barrel in the hall for the used toilet paper. The family proudly served a meal of BBQ. I found out later, the BBQ meat was probably dog or cat. The poverty throughout Mexico was shocking to me.

I came home to a troubled environment. My mother, brother, and I lived in a small apartment with two dogs. My sister moved to live with my father. One time, when my mother and brother were gone; I was date raped. The young man kept refilling my wine glass and committed this horrendous act of bullying.

For my student teaching assignment, I taught Honors Spanish. I was assigned to a teacher who introduced herself as part of a mafia family. I don't understand why she felt the need to intimidate me. She allowed me to teach one class and she forbade me to go to the staff lounge for lunch. I found out too late; I could have petitioned for a change in supervisor.

My only remaining quarter of study was during the winter quarter. I lived off campus in a room off the side of an older couples' home. My roommates were Chinese graduate students and they were rarely around the house. I maintained a 4.0 GPA, despite suffering from an ulcer.

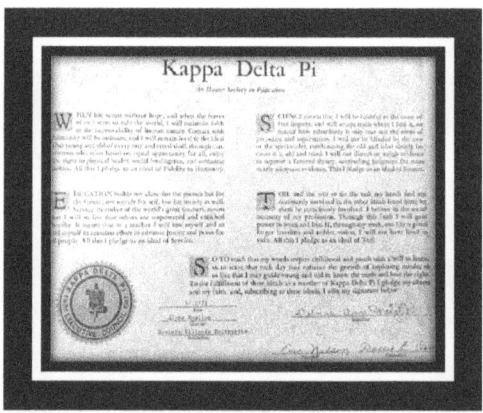

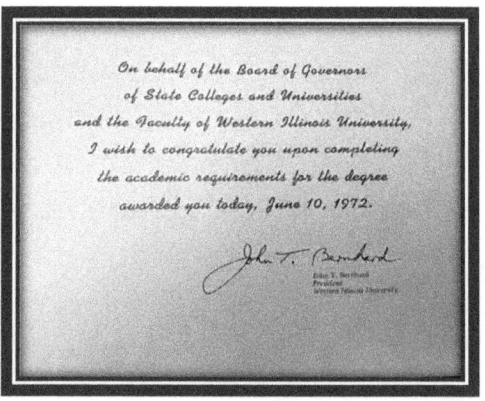

I graduated one quarter early Magna Cum Laude with a Bachelor of Arts in Education: Spanish (major) and Drama (minor). I was accepted into two honorary societies: Alpha Mu Gamma (foreign language) and Kappa Delta Pi (education).

I was the first in my family to earn a college degree. Despite my visual disability, I was able to climb this mountain, against all odds!

Since was a shortage of teaching jobs and I was not Hispanic; I could not obtain a teaching job as a high school Spanish teacher. I was very apprehensive! I had a car loan and a room in the upstairs of an old home to pay for every month.

I started tutoring in reading comprehension. Tutoring was a joy and became a life-long passion of helping others. I also worked as a substitute teacher. In addition, I worked as a file clerk at a Semi-Conductor Specialists. A co-worker spoke about New Zealand and Australia. This part of the world remains on my "bucket list".

I did not work as a clerk very long because my father offered me a job at the company where he worked. My job was a "Girl Friday" or secretary in the front office. I loved the variety and being around my dad almost every day.

I was distressed about the injustice happening around the world.

If I Had my Way

If I had my way, all peoples would live in peace.

If I had my way, starvation would be out of reach.

If I had my way, every country would have free speech.

PERCEPTION, RECOGNITION, APPRECIATION,

Sadly, we live in a world that's broken.

Folks who hate others are outspoken.

Parents and children are heartbroken.

DISPIRITED, DISTURBED, DISAPPOINTED

We need to return to compassion.

The brave must demand a commission.

A courageous and empathetic expedition.

ALTERNESS, RECEPTIVENESS, REPONSIVENESS

If I had my way, we'd take to the streets today.

If I had my way, we'd make progress day by day.

If I had my way, kindness wouldn't be one way.

*GET ON UP, MOVE RIGHT OUT, LEND A
HAND*

*Let's fight prejudice with shared
understanding.*

Let's battle bullying by confidence building.

Let's work together loving and forgiving.

*CONSIDERATE, SYMPATHETIC,
COMPASSIONATE*

No longer can there be hate.

We need our priorities straight.

Relate, advocate, motivate.

*IF I HAD MY WAY, PEACE WOULD HAVE
A CHANCE!*

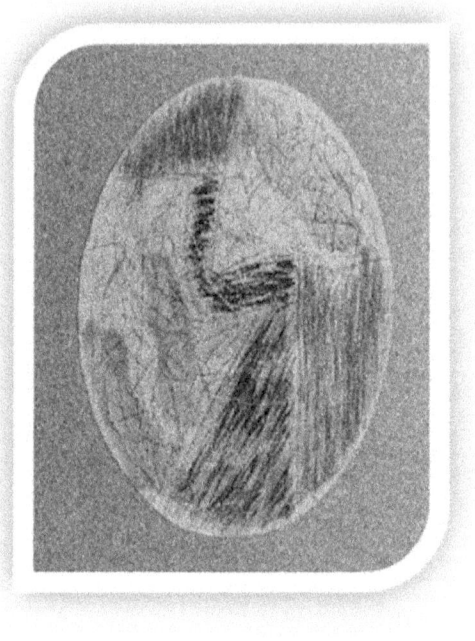

Perseverance

I am still a child.

I have so much more to learn, so much more to experience.

I am constantly searching, constantly questioning.

Won't anyone help?

Can't anyone help?

NO.

I must find the world myself, find my mind myself.

I have a long road to travel, a high hill to climb.

I won't give up.

I can't give up.

WHY?

Because if I do, I will cease to exist and will never grow up.

There are always CONFLICTS, RESTRICTIONS, INDECISIVENESS.

So many feeling are present yet FEAR enters in.

FEAR of being hurt, becoming involved, hurting another, ONESELF.

I have found a new relationship – one primarily of the mind, FRESH, which my emotions would like to make STALE.

All need warmth, love, security, protection YET because of others around them, A HALT.

So many warm feelings would like to be showered, shared.

Once love was sweet – then bitter, shut off.

Will it come again? Will it grow now?

Will I ruin an understanding with love?

Life is a riddle that constantly changes its answer and makes man question his soul at every turn.

Chapter Twelve: True Love at Last

On 2/12/1973, I wrote this poem to Jim.

It's strange to be analyzing another regarding his life and yours.

When someone occurs in my life, why should I constantly: play a game of pro and con?

I enjoy being with him is that not enough?

I do not wish to change his personality or soul.

I constantly think about him: events and thoughtful things he does.

His handsome face and "bod".

How he could enhance his own good looks.

Of course thoughts about sex enter in.

Will he still care when he knows I am old-fashioned?

I've heard some sex is fine, but too much ruins a relationship.

*What does he like: modern décor,
Mediterranean, contemporary?*

*I know (like me) that he enjoys: plays,
dinner out, running, nature, poetry, calm
music, rock (once in a while), non-violence,
ice cream, movies, spiritual.*

*But, does he like: ballet, dancing,
yogurt (I think so), waffles, rainbows,
horseback riding?*

*Does he feel children should have a
good religious background?*

*I know he enjoys prayer, but would
he like my church?*

So many questions.

Does he have any?

I'm sure he does.

*You're strong and gentle; quiet and loud;
complimenting and criticizing; gay and
serious.*

Because you are a man.

*Your appearance is "straight", but your
mind is "semi".*

Who knows what the future will hold.

Will we "get together"; decide it's just or fun; split up?

I will trust in God and know He will do the best for both of us.

Whatever happens, Jim, you are a unique individual and I do care.

Let's let time be our teacher and God be our guide.

In April, 1973, I became engaged to a handsome and kind young man; whom I had met years ago in the summer of 1968.

This awesome, quiet man married a dramatic, energic woman in June, 1973. We began our life together in the small hamlet of Carol Stream, IL. We had planned to get married in October; however, after my elderly landlord made a pass at me, I needed to move out immediately.

Our wedding plans went into high gear. Our friends and family fully supported our decision and we planned a simple civil ceremony. A small gathering with family, friends, and our pastor happened a month later.

If you saw us walking along, you may think; how do they go together? Jim stood over six feet tall and I was under five feet. I had long and wavy dark blonde hair and he had short and curly brown hair, with red highlights.

Our core beliefs were similar. We were raised in the same area of the country during the same years. After many hours of conversation; we both agreed we wanted four children. Ironically, in college, many of my friends wanted to adopt two children and have two biological children. We were in love and remain best friends.

The following poem was written on 10/16/73 – our four-month anniversary.

With you, I feel complete and content.

Without you, I feel alone and alienated.

These past four months have been heavenly to me. You are the best think that has happened in my life.

I know that our life will be full of wonderful events and growth will be mutual and profitable for both of us.

Sometimes I am very trying.

Sometimes I do not bring you joy.

Sometimes I do not enjoy all that I should.

FORGIVE ME.

I thank you for helping me mentally, physically, and spiritually.

*I do hope that I have done the same
for you.*

*I do so want to make you happy
and content.*

No matter what anyone else

says,

does,

thinks,

sees,

or feels:

I LOVE YOU.

Happy Anniversary Dearest One.

Although we wanted to start a family as soon as possible; we were surprised I was pregnant on our first anniversary. Unfortunately, I miscarried my fifth week. My doctor blamed "old" eggs from being on birth control for a few months.

It was a mixed blessing because we were devastated at the loss; however, Jim now knew he could become a father. His coach did not have biological children and he was worried he would not be able to be a father.

I was apprehensive because of our loss; our size difference as a couple; and the fact my mother had a Caesarian Section or C-Section. After months of fertility counseling; we found out I was pregnant and due in January of 1976.

When I found out I was pregnant, I was working as a bi-lingual secretary with a talented lady, Yolly. We made a plaque for Yolly and Ray as a token of our friendship. We started families at the same time and have kept in touch throughout the decades.

Chapter Thirteen: Progeny

David was born two weeks past my due date via C-Section, after forty-four hours of labor. Dave weighed seven pounds and twelve ounces. We were overjoyed to bring him home to West Chicago, formerly Turner Junction.

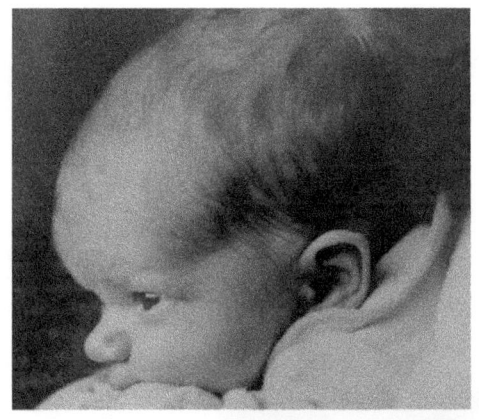

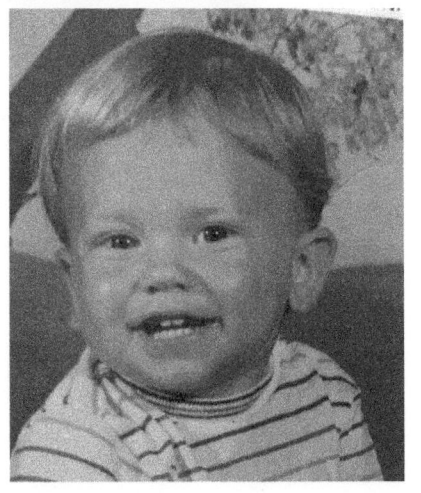

Two and one-half years later, we brought home a beautiful, tiny daughter, Rebekah. The doctor recommended another C-Section because of our size difference as a couple. She was born on her due date in July, 1978; however, we remained in the hospital for a week. She was jaundice and her weight had dropped under six pounds. She was a content baby, who slept often.

After Bekah's first birthday, we moved into a house we had built in St. Charles, a lovely town on the Fox River. The house in West Chicago with two bedrooms and one bathroom was small and we wanted more children. My doctors advised me not have more than three children. Too many epidurals could leave me paralyzed.

Fortunately, I got pregnant soon and was due in June of 1980. My mother told me to have an abortion because she did not want me to go through another surgery. According to our beliefs, abortion was not an option. We consulted with our pastor and doctor and decided to move forward. A tubal ligation after the birth was the best course for us.

Precious Leah was born two weeks later in July of 1980. I had a lot of Braxton Hicks labor and she was almost born the night before her scheduled delivery. This time, Jim was able to observe the delivery. Amazingly, he did not faint!

We are tremendously grateful to have such incredible children! Our offspring have brought us many hours of joy.

When our children were still at home, we had good times together throughout Chicagoland. In addition, we took vacations in WI, FL, NC, and HI.

We are extremely proud of the awesome adults they have become.

August 2014

Chapter Fourteen: Teaching

While still living in St. Charles, we learned the public school near us pioneered every new program the district piloted. Consequently, we helped start a Christian school in Geneva.

I taught second grade at the Christian school and the children attended there for many years. I found joy in teaching second grade and adapting a high school Spanish curriculum for junior high students. On the first day of school, I told parents to be on the lookout for the Spanish and sign-language words their children would learn.

While teaching in Geneva, we decided to build a bigger home, using the same builder we had in St. Charles. It was our dream house on a large lot on the edge of town. We loved watching the sunsets over the farm fields. We adopted an fabulous huskie/lab mix named D.J. or Dr. Juggles from a fellow teacher. He filled our life with joy for about ten years.

We visited Hawaii on our fourteenth anniversary as a delayed honeymoon, using my entire annual salary. Later, after Jim's mother died in 1988; we took the kids to Hawaii in her honor.

I decided it was time to leave my position at the school and Jim was looking for work in Hawaii. Unfortunately, the Hawaiian opportunity did not work out. We would have lived in poverty with three budding teens. In addition, D.J. would have to be quarantined for a year.

I took a few years off from full-time teaching and continued to work as a tutor out of my home. Additionally, I taught Spanish to the administration and English to the factory workers, at the company where Jim worked.

I became active in politics and theater as well. The local newspaper featured my business and I was thrilled! I have always been passionate about helping others achieve their best.

My size and visual challenges did not hold me back!

Debby Hackbarth of Hackbarth Educational Language Pronunciation Services (H.E.L.P.S.) reads to her students in her home office in her basement. She established H.E.L.P.S. to expand her work as a teacher and tutor.

Bob Gerrard/Chronicle photo staff

I started attending Northern Illinois University (NIU) while working part-time as a teacher and tutor; doing volunteer work as a precinct captain; and serving on the board of the local library. I needed to quit performing in community theater. In three years, I achieved two separate Master's Degrees in Education (Special Education) and Reading (Literacy). I moved from special education teaching to working as a Reading Specialist.

I served on the Geneva Public Library Board thanks to the encouragement from a friend, Dick Sharp. I ended my tenure as Vice President.

My husband and my mother were present at my graduation from NIU. Imagine, a tiny premature wonder who couldn't read, receiving a Master's Degree in Reading!

Chapter Fifteen: Big Changes

After living in Illinois for over forty years, we made the difficult decision to move to the Seattle area. We left family and fantastic friends, who opened the world of the deaf culture to me. One of my best friends, Sue, said I could be her ears and she would be my eyes. I learned to sign and used both Spanish and sign at the same time; while chatting with friends.

Jim and I cherish the friendship we have maintained with Sue and her husband, Gary. We wish we could get together more often. They are avid travelers and devoted parents and grandparents. They visited us in TX and AL and we visited them in CO. In their honor, I named two characters in my books after them.

Never let an handicapping condition hold you back from enjoying life to the fullest! Sue, Gary, and I are perfect examples of success stories in a world where being "outside the norm" is often not honored.

TX

AL

CO

There were several reasons for a move out of IL. We were weary of the cold weather; neither one of us were satisfied with our jobs; I missed a friend who was like a sister to me, Debi; Jim's relatives lived there; and one of our children wanted to go to college in WA.

Deb and Debi

Right after the school year ended, Bekah and I drove out to Deming, WA; so that I could seek employment. On our first stop, we enjoyed buying some new shoes! The drive was challenging; however, we had a great time together. Bekah needed to do all of the night driving because I have night-blindness, due to my low vision.

I lived with Debi and her family while I searched for a job in special education or as a reading specialist. I looked throughout the Seattle area. Jim came out to visit me once during my hunt because we had been apart too long.

After a few weeks, I secured employment in special education with the Highline District. We were on our way!

Jim and our kids got the house ready to sell. I came back to IL after seven weeks to help "weed out" our belongings and to pack up. After we put the house on the market; it took months to sell the house.

Two of our children stayed in IL in college and one came with us to finish the final year of high school. It was a hectic, stressful, and exciting time!

Section Sixteen: Washington

Because our new jobs paid at the end of the month; we did not have any income for over a month. The move was difficult financially, emotionally, and physically.

In WA, I loved living an hour from the ocean; driving through the foothills to work; and eating salmon often. We made fabulous friends, Leroy and Cathy, while living in the Fairwood area of Renton, WA.

Leroy and Cathy

Years later, we visited them in Las Vegas. We had a great meal together at one of their favorite restaurants. They showed us the breathtaking Red Rock Canyon in the Mojave Desert.

outside the restaurant

at Red Rock Canyon

I chose to avoid politics and theater and focus on my career. I taught students with special needs in a junior high school close to the inner city for a year. Toward the end of the year, my principal recommended me for the District Literacy Team, as the Head Reading Specialist. I was honored to have been asked to serve the district in this capacity. I welcomed the change because I had been assaulted by one of my students

I loved working at the district level as a specialist because I created classes for teachers; worked alongside teachers in their classrooms; and attended many state-wide literacy events. I could make my own hours and came and went as I pleased!

While the administrative team was examining a district-wide curriculum adoption; the team leader suggested I start earning an administrative credential. She saw how well I worked with adults. Consequently, I started taking classes through Central Washington University (CWU) and obtained certification in administration. In retrospect, I wish I had taken a few extra classes and obtained a third Master's Degree.

Unfortunately, the monies for the literacy job dried up and a principal who decided to move districts wanted me to move with her. The Lake Washington School District was the home of Microsoft. The new environment was decidedly different, but also challenging. I finished my studies at CWU and began working as an Assistant Principal; while still serving students with special needs. The principals with whom I worked were great mentors.

A year after we lost D.J.; we were overjoyed to adopt another loving dog, Holly. We took Holly on our hikes in the forest.

Chapter Seventeen: Texas

As much as we loved living in the northwest, another change was on the horizon. We visited Austin and loved the area when we were asked for assistance from one of our children. Jim was able to secure employment with a local utility company. Within three months, we moved to a home in Cedar Park, TX, a northwest suburb of Austin. We loved the hill country outside of Austin because it reminded us of the northwest.

I did not work for a few months while we settled in our new home. After passing the state test in administration; my dentist suggested I apply for the elementary principalship at the Christian school close to his practice. In our teens, the dentist and I met at our mutual orthodontist! I got the job and loved working there. I was overjoyed to start a program for students with special needs and provide staff development.

After my time at the school ended, I worked for Pearson and then for the City of Austin in the Code Department. While at Pearson, one of my colleagues confirmed a suspicion I had for years. She had worked with students with dyslexia and she assured me I was dyslexic.

Actually, I was relieved because I thought some of my communication difficulties were cognitive; however, they were due to dyslexia. Throughout my life, I have reversed letters when reading and numbers when I am fatigued.

Many marvelous miracles have happened for me as a dyslexic. I served as a Reading Specialist, a District Reading Expert, and I was able to obtain two Master's Degrees. while maturing into a Master Teacher. Furthermore, amazing as it may seem; I am a visual learner! I need to write down information, after it's told to me auditorily.

Our beautiful home in Cedar Park, TX was located on a golf course, close to the hill country. We joined a golf club there and enjoyed golfing for many years.

from the front

out the back

Over the years, Jim and I have loved playing sports together. We went on many bicycle trips and hiked frequently when we lived in WA. Now, in TX, we golfed every week.

Because of our height, Jim needed to have his clubs lengthened while mine were shortened! I had trouble in my short game and putting because I have no depth perception. Golf lessons and a patient husband helped tremendously. I didn't mind the challenges of playing golf because we were spending time outside together on an outstanding golf course.

While living in Cedar Park, I met a gal who continues to be a terrific friend, Karen. We spent many hours talking about our leadership roles while we hiked around the neighborhood.

Like me, her tiny stature never held her back. We are both survivors: she is in remission from cancer and I have overcome repeated bullying and criticism. Don't let people tell you tasks are impossible!

After we moved to TX, Cathy and Leroy came out to visit us. We decided to introduce them to our new friends, Karen and Burton. We took an unforgettable excursion to the River Walk of San Antonio. Everyone had an exceptional time of laughing, eating, and sightseeing.

Cathy, Deb, Karen – San Antonio

It took fourteen years, but we moved closer to the deep waters again.

Chapter Eighteen: Alabama

While in WA, we were about an hour from the Pacific Ocean.

In AL, we live about three miles from Mobile Bay and about an hour from the Gulf of Mexico.

I love the sound of waves.

We're loving living in Fairhope. The utopian colony established in 1894 gave its citizens a "fair hope of success". This is how Fairhope got its name.

the iconic Fairhope clock

In 2019, my friends and I planned a Christmas party for the neighborhood. At that event, we met Henry and Toni. I am very grateful to be taking piano lessons from an outstanding and compassionate teacher, Toni.

One day when we were discussing some difficulties I was having; she asked if I have dyslexia. I told her about my history and she has been very calm and patient with me. She has been amazed at my progress throughout the years. Toni and Henry are dear friends.

Jim, Deb, Toni, and Henry

With my daughter's encouragement, I started to work out at Pure Barre in 2015. In TX, I completed five-hundred and eight classes and in AL, I finished five-hundred classes. Because I have limited peripheral vision on my left side; I could not observe the instructor when she was on my left. However, I kept on going with the encouragement from family and friends

I was blessed to work out alongside our daughters, in different states, at different studios, throughout the years. A very special time happened when our daughter, Bekah, was the instructor when Leah and I made our 250th class! It was a complete surprise to me when this happened! I was concentrating too hard on trying to execute all of the positions, for any tears of joy. Those happy tears came later.

I kept working out even after having a meniscus tear repaired on my left knee and a cyst removed from my left wrist. I frequently ponder if my left side was not fully developed due to my premature birth.

Leesburg, instructor Bekah

TX with Dave, my 500th class.

AL with Jim, my 500th class

I had the meniscus tear repaired after trying one Taekwondo class. Years of tap dancing had laid the groundwork for the meniscus tear. I used the work outs at Pure Barre to strengthen the muscles around my knee, as well as my entire body.

My doctors and friends were shocked when they found out Jim and I had started a journey in Mixed Martial Arts at Invictus Martial Arts in August of 2020.

On July, 15, 2023, Jim and I received our first Dan black belts in Kick Boxing/MMA at Invictus Martial Arts in Austin. Jim and I were the most senior in our class. Fantastic teaching and mentorship, with lots of practice, helped us reach this milestone. All of our classes have been taken remotely. We hope to continue our journey for many years.

It was a blessing and honor to receive our black belts alongside our grandson. Our son awarded our belts to us, which caused a grateful tear. My friend, Karen, who now lives in CO and KY, attended the ceremony. She went out of her way to fly to Austin to celebrate with us.

Jim and Deb at the ceremony

Dave, Deb, Jim, Jonah, Mrs. Garza

Chapter Nineteen: "Retired"

This quilt, made by my friend in WA, Debi, hangs in our office. The quilt is a reminder of the years I have worked in the field of education. In this room, I write, draw, and tutor. I started writing in third grade; drawing in high school; working with elementary students while in high school; and tutoring when I got out of college. I'm retired, but not idle!

The idea for Fairhope Dragon series began from a short story I wrote in 2012. The books were written in 2022 and 2023. Samples of the books' artwork are shown below.

Grandson Carter's art

Grandson Jonah's art

Debby's art

To find out more about the books, scan the QR code above and read the testimonies.

For thirteen years, I have waited for the unconditional love a dog can offer. My chiropractor told me about a wonderful kennel in Robertsdale, AL and we adopted an eight-year-old former breeder. She is well-loved in our home and acts half her age, most of the time. This is Farrah.

Chapter Twenty: Jim, Beloved

We met when I was seventeen and he was eighteen. We dated for a few months and had two further dates. We did not marry until we were twenty-two and twenty-three, after college.

After we were married, he told me he wanted to be with me since our first date. Although we were very far apart in size and personality; we had the same values and beliefs. We reaffirmed our commitment to Christ at the same time in 1974. Plus, we had a similar taste in music!

Jim has been my "rock" throughout my lifetime. He calms me when I get frustrated because I cannot see well. Often, I bump into walls and items on my left side. When the print is very small, he will read to me. The majority of the time, he drives places, especially at night.

I've told him in jest, he can never die because I would not be able to reach anything. I hope we are together to the very end, due to our mutual devotion.

We are dedicated to our children and grandchildren and have told each one of them of our unconditional love.

Dynamic Debby

Blessed times together for fifty years.

Trips	Comments
Palco & Hays, KS; Omaha, NE	Job interview; honeymoon night
Washington Island, WI	1st anniversary; Viking culture
Elkhorn, WI	Lu's trailer; Jim's Aunt Lil's home
Kauai, HI	1987 (14th anniversary): 1991 (entire family)
Headford, Ireland	30th anniversary; castles; cemeteries
Vancouver, Canada	Bouchart Gardens; Empress Hotel
Nueva Vallarta, Mexico	Puerta Vallarta; mariachis
CA; OR	40th anniversary; Humboldt County; OR Dunes
Las Vegas, NV	Cathy/Leroy
CO	Genessee (Karen); Littleton (Sue/Gary)
Inside Passage, AK	50th anniversary: 1st cruise; glaciers & whales

Music/Theater	Comments
Arie Crown Theater - Chicago, IL	Yul Brynner - Home Sweet Homer; King & I
Ravinia – Highland Park, IL	John Denver
Theater - Chicago	Santana
Candlelight Dinner Playhouse – Summit, IL	Man of La Mancha; Fiddler on the Roof; 1776
Pheasant Run – St. Charles, IL	3 on a Mattress – Jerry Stiller
Paramount-Seattle	Cats; Annie
Jazz Alley - Seattle	Lee Ritenour; David Benoit
Chateau Ste. Michelle – Woodinville, WA	David Benoir, The Moody Blues
Theater - Seattle	Bryan Culbertson
Marymoor Park - Redmond, WA	The Moody Blues
One World Theater – Austin, TX	Bryan Culbertson; Fourplay; Peter White; Keiko Matsui
Austin City Limits	The Moody Blues
Cedar Park Center	The Moody Blues
Las Vegas, NV	Blue Man Group

Ireland

Mexico

California

Texas

Colorado

Alaska

Remember, you never know the path your life will take. Life and marriage can be challenging

Follow your dreams; don't let life's challenges stop you.

Jim will always be my best friend.

Epilogue

How did a small town midwestern girl end up in the beautiful village of Fairhope? My family was involved in the development of the state of Illinois as the first governor and as the first settlers in Geneva and Rockford. The state of Alabama was not on my radar growing up enveloped by corn fields. However, the move to Alabama was a culmination of hopes and dreams over many decades, with a continuing faith in God.

When my great aunt, who was like a grandma to me, moved to Florida in 1969, I knew I wanted to live close to her in the south, surrounded by sand not farmers' fields. Although the closest large body of water was Lake Michigan, fifty miles away, I really wanted to relocate to be near the water. However, I put the dream aside to pursue another dream of becoming an educator and then marrying my best friend. Then wonderous children came upon the scene, a handsome son and two gorgeous daughters.

It took twenty-eight years, but I finally left the frozen tundra or the Chicago area. My soul felt alive when we settled in the Seattle area for ten years. The lush green fern-filled forests sang to me every day. We hiked often and made a way to visit the peaceful ocean at least once a year. Unfortunately, the weather rarely warmed up past the sixties and jobs were not as we had planned.

Finally, in 2005, we made our way to Texas for a warmer climate and to be close to our only surviving grandchild. All along the way, I was fortunate enough to keep helping students to achieve their best as a professional tutor and mentor. We started visiting Fairhope and decided to move to the utopian paradise as soon as possible.

We are delighted to live in this vibrant colony, close to family and new friends. In addition to continuing to help students; I now publish books and create unique pieces of art. This artwork is sold at charming establishments from Fairhope to Robertsdale.

I am thrilled to be part of the active artist communities located on the Eastern Shore of Mobile Bay and in the countryside of Baldwin County.

For the past few years, I have served our colony as the editor and a contributing author for the colony newsletter, *The Fairhopers*. Recently, my peers in Pensters Writing Group have selected me as their secretary.

Every day is a miracle to this tiny preemie with visual challenges. I hope to continue to passionately inspire others to keep following their dreams.

I believe, with every fiber of my being, every person can learn and thrive. If I can be what I am today – a black belt in martial arts and an author and artist - anyone can achieve the best life has to offer.

Tiny preemies with visual challenges can do anything!

Do the words I express

have importance

for others?

I have faith in mankind

and

love for all around me.

Life is not enjoyed

until

you find yourself.

Acknowledgments

For a long time, I thought about writing a memoir. Rosanne Gulisano sparked the flame through her inspiring words and gifted mentorship. Alan Samry's memoir and Deborah McDonald's books painted talented canvases for guidance. John O'Melveny Woods has inspired and lead me through the writing process. My husband, Jim, has continued to patiently help me to improve my work. A huge thanks to each one of you.

I would not be the "tiny tornado" without the genetic gifts and support of my parents throughout my life. God has always watched over me and blessed me with many different abilities; even though I did not recognize them for many years. My loving family and friends have always been there for me, in good times and bad times.

Thank you.

Made in the USA

Debby Hackbarth

www.ingramcontent.com/pod-product-compliance
Lightning Source LLC
Chambersburg PA
CBHW042316120626
46547CB00022B/2170